A Mother's Prayers for Her Child in the Military

21 Days to Trust God from Afar

Ivelisse Adorno

Kitvi Editorial, LLC

Copyright Page

DEDICATION

For Gla

For the brave mother who has learned to turn worry into
prayer and distance into faith.

May every page of this book remind you that God
watches over your child, even when you cannot see him,
and that while you pray, God is always at work.

Behind every child who serves, there is a mother who prays.

Table of Contents

Introduction

There are worries that are never spoken out loud. They settle in the chest, quietly circle the mind, and show up at the most unexpected moments of the day. That is often the daily reality of a mother whose child serves far from home.

It's not always about something that is happening. Sometimes it's the imagination, the silence, a piece of news—or simply love itself, which, when it cannot protect through closeness, tries to do so through thought.

This collection of prayers was born from a very real place. It came from watching my sister cry, hearing the heaviness in her voice as she worried about her child, and feeling—as her sister—the weight of not being able to do anything... except pray.

In that moment, I understood something clearly: there are battles that are not won through control, but through surrender. Because even though a mother loves deeply, there is a kind of care that only God can give. And that is where this book finds its purpose.

You won't find perfect answers here, nor empty promises that everything will be easy. But you will find a space to breathe, to pray, and to remember that you are not alone.

Faith doesn't always remove anxiety—but it can transform it. It can take what troubles the heart and carry it into a place of rest in God.

Each day of this book offers a simple invitation: bring your child before God once again, and allow your own heart to be cared for in the process. Because while you are thinking of your child, God is watching over him. And while you pray, God is still at work.

Day 1

When the Mind Imagines the Worst

Philippians 4:6-7

"God reminds us that we don't have to live in anxiety. Instead, we can bring everything to Him in prayer, trusting that His peace will guard our hearts and our minds."

Being the mother of someone who serves far from home can bring moments of deep worry. Many times, it isn't what is actually happening that troubles your heart—it's what your mind begins to imagine.

A long silence, a news report, or a sudden thought can quickly turn into a story in your mind, filling your heart with fear.

If you've ever found yourself thinking this way, it doesn't mean you lack faith. It simply means you love deeply. A mother's love always wants to protect—even when distance makes that impossible.

God understands that kind of love. He sees the heart of a mother who wishes she could be close enough to keep her child safe.

That's why we are not called to ignore our worries, but to bring them to God. Every fearful thought can become a prayer. Every anxious moment can become a reminder that God sees your child, even when you cannot.

Today, you don't need to have all the answers. You only need to remember this: while you are thinking about your child, God is already taking care of him.

Prayer

Lord,
when my mind begins to imagine the worst, help me remember that You are already watching over my child. Protect him wherever he is, guide every step he takes, and fill my heart with Your peace. Today, I place his life in Your hands once again.

Amen.

Declaration

Today I choose to trust God's care over my child.

My prayer for my child today:

Day 2

When Silence Makes the Heart Uneasy

Psalm 46:1
"God is our refuge and strength, an ever-present help in trouble."

There are moments when silence can unsettle a mother's heart. Maybe the phone hasn't rung, maybe hours have passed without hearing from your child, and your mind begins to fill with questions. Your heart simply wants to know that everything is okay.

In those moments, the imagination can start working faster than it should. The mind tries to fill the silence with assumptions that don't always reflect reality.

But silence does not always mean danger. Many times, it simply means life is moving forward—responsibilities, long shifts, busy days, and moments when there is no chance to call.

God does not depend on updates to know how your child is doing. He doesn't need calls, messages, or reports to see every step your child takes.

Where your child is right now, God is already there.

While you wait here, God is there. While the silence feels long to you, there is no uncertainty for Him.

Today, you can choose to let that silence become not a space of fear, but a reminder that God's care is still active— even when you don't know what is happening.

Your child is never outside of God's hands.

Prayer

Lord,
when silence makes me uneasy and my mind begins to worry, help me remember that You are caring for my child. Protect him wherever he is, guide his steps, and fill me with Your peace as I trust in Your care.

Amen.

Declaration

Even in the silence, God is caring for my child.

My prayer for my child today:

Day 3

Letting Go of What I Can't Control

Psalm 121:3-4
"He will not let your foot slip—He who watches over you will not slumber; indeed, He who watches over Israel will neither slumber nor sleep."

There are things, as a mother, you wish you could control.
You want to know exactly where your child is at all times—what they're doing, who they're with—and you wish nothing harmful could ever come near them.
That desire comes from love.

But there comes a point in life when that control is no longer possible.
And when a child is serving far away, that reality feels even heavier.

A mother's heart wants to stay alert at all times—watching, checking, staying aware of everything.
But living that way can become exhausting.

God never gets tired.

While you sleep, He is watching.
While you work, He is still caring.
While you pray, He is already moving.

Letting go of control does not mean you love less.
It means recognizing that there is a greater care than your own.

Today, you can take what worries you and place it in
God's hands once again.
He is never distracted, never mistaken, and never loses
sight of those He loves.

Your child is under the constant care of a God who never
sleeps.

Prayer

Lord,
today I recognize that there are things I cannot control.
I place my child's life in Your hands.
Protect them, guide them, and watch over every step they
take.
Help me rest in Your care and trust that You are always
watching over them.
Amen.

Declaration

God is watching over my child at all times.

Today, I place my child before You in prayer:

Day 4

When the Heart Fills with "What Ifs..."

Matthew 6:34
"Therefore do not worry about tomorrow, for tomorrow will worry about itself. Each day has enough trouble of its own."

Sometimes it all begins with a small question:
"What if...?"

What if something happens?
What if they're in danger?
What if something occurs that I can't prevent?

Before you realize it, that question begins to grow forming a chain of thoughts that fills your heart with uneasiness.

When the mind loves deeply, it tries to get ahead of any possible pain. But most of the time, it does so by imagining the worst.

Jesus understood this tendency of the human heart. That's why He taught something so simple, yet so powerful: to live one day at a time.

Today, you don't need to carry tomorrow.
Today, you don't need to solve what hasn't happened.

Your child has a today.
And God is with them in that today.

Tomorrow has not yet arrived—but when it does, God will
be there too.

Today, you can release those "what ifs"
and rest in God's care for this moment.

Prayer

Lord,
when my mind fills with questions and "what ifs,"
help me return to the present.

Today, I place my child in Your hands.
Watch over them wherever they are,
and fill me with Your peace so I can trust You one day at a
time. Amen.

Declaration

Today, I trust God—one day at a time.

Today, I bring this before You for my child:

Day 5

God Knows Exactly Where Your Child Is

Psalm 139:7–10
"Where can I go from Your Spirit? Where can I flee from Your presence? If I go up to the heavens, You are there..."

There are moments when the hardest part isn't what's happening it's not knowing exactly where your child is or what they're doing.

When they were younger, you knew everything. Where they were, what they were doing, when they would return.

Now there is distance. And sometimes, that distance is felt more in the heart than in the miles. But there is a truth that brings rest: You may not know exactly where your child is right now, but God does.

There is no base, no city, no border, no mission that is outside of God's presence.

He sees every step, every place, and every moment.

Where your child is right now,
God is there.

There is no distance for Him. No place too far. No moment outside of His care. Today, you can rest in this truth: your child is never beyond God's reach.

Prayer

Lord,
thank You because You know exactly where my child is
today.
No place is far from Your presence.

I ask that You protect them, guide them, and be with
them wherever they are.
Help me rest in Your care. Amen.

Declaration

God is with my child wherever they are.

Today, I entrust my child into Your care:

Day 6

When the Heart Grows Tired of Worrying

1 Peter 5:7
"Cast all your anxiety on Him because He cares for you."

There are days when worry is not just a passing thought, but a constant weight.

It follows you through the day. Returns at night. And lingers longer than you wish it would. A mother's love runs deep, and because of that, the mind tries to get ahead of any possible danger.

But living in that constant state of alert can exhaust the heart. God understands that kind of weariness. That's why He doesn't ask us to ignore anxiety-He invites us to give it to Him.

To place something in God's hands means recognizing that we are not meant to carry everything alone.

It's saying:
"Lord, this worries me…
but I place it in Your hands
because I know You care better than I ever could."

Today, you can release that thought that keeps returning again and again. And maybe tomorrow, you'll need to do it again.

And that's okay.

Trust is often not a one-time act, but a daily decision.

Prayer

Lord,
You know the worries I carry in my heart. Today, I place
them in Your hands. Watch over my child wherever they
are, and help me rest in Your care. Fill my heart with Your
peace
as I learn to trust You day by day. Amen.

Declaration

Today, I release my worries to God.

Today, I surrender my worries to You for my child:

Day 7

When Faith and Fear Walk Together

Isaiah 41:10
"Do not fear, for I am with you; do not be dismayed, for I am your God."

Sometimes we think that having faith means not feeling fear. But the truth is, many times faith and fear walk side by side for a while.

You can trust God and still feel worried. You can have faith and still feel uneasiness in your heart. That doesn't mean your faith is weak-it means you are human. God does not step away when we feel afraid; He draws near. His presence does not depend on our hearts being perfectly calm. Faith doesn't always remove fear right away, but it does teach us where to look when fear shows up. Today, you don't have to wait until you feel completely at peace to trust God. You can come just as you are. And little by little, as you choose to trust, peace begins to take up more space than fear.

Prayer

Lord,
sometimes I feel worried about my child, but today I choose to bring everything in my heart to You.

Strengthen my faith, fill me with Your peace, and watch over my child wherever they are.

Thank You because You are with me even in the middle of my fears. Amen.

Declaration

My faith is stronger than my fear because God is with me.

Today, I bring both my faith and my fears before You for my child:

Day 8

When You Need to Remember
Your Child Is Not Alone

Joshua 1:9
"Be strong and courageous. Do not be afraid; do not be discouraged, for the Lord your God will be with you wherever you go."

There is something that deeply aches in a mother's heart: the thought that her child is far away... and alone.

That image can appear without warning. Your mind begins to imagine where they are, how they are, whether someone is watching over them, whether someone is there for them.

But there is a truth greater than any thought:

Your child is never alone You may not be there physically. You may not be able to see them or speak to them at all times.

But God is.

Where your child walks, God walks.
Where your child rests, God is present.
Where your child faces challenges, God holds them.

There is no shift, no mission, no border, no place where God's presence cannot reach them.

Today, instead of imagining loneliness, you can remember presence.

Your child is accompanied by the One who never leaves.

Prayer

Lord,
when my heart feels like my child is alone, remind me that You are with them. Walk with them in every step, protect them, and surround them with Your presence. Help me rest in the assurance that You never leave them. Amen.

Declaration

My child is never alone God is with them.

Today, I place my child in Your presence:

Day 9

When the News Disturbs Your Heart

Psalm 112:7
"They will have no fear of bad news; their hearts are steadfast, trusting in the Lord."

We live in a world where news travels fast and often, it does not bring peace. A headline, a video, a story someone shares and suddenly, your heart tightens.

Without even realizing it, you begin to connect what you see with your child. The mind starts forming connections that only increase the worry.

But not everything you hear is what your child is experiencing.

The news reflects real situations, yes but it can also amplify fear when it is not filtered through faith. God does not want you to live reacting to every piece of information. He wants your heart to be grounded in something more stable than any headline: His presence.

Your peace does not depend on what the media says. It depends on who you choose to trust.

Today, you can choose not to feed fear with information you cannot control but to feed your faith with the truth that God is still watching over your child.

Prayer

Lord,
when I hear news that unsettles my heart, help me not to
be led by fear. Remind me that You are in control and that
You are caring for my child at all times. Fill my heart with
trust in You. Amen.

Declaration

My heart is steady because I trust in God.

**Today, I choose to trust You over what I hear about my
child:**

Day 10

When Pride and Worry
Live in the Same Heart

Psalm 20:7
"Some trust in chariots and some in horses, but we trust in the name of the Lord our God."

There is a feeling many mothers experience but do not always know how to name. On one hand, there is pride. Pride in what your child is doing, in their courage, and in their willingness to serve. But at the same time, there is worry—a quiet, constant concern that is not always spoken out loud.

Sometimes both emotions live together in the same heart. You feel proud, but also vulnerable. Grateful, but still uneasy. God is not asking you to choose one or the other. He understands both.

You can honor your child's purpose and still bring your concerns before God. You do not have to hide what you feel in order to appear strong. True strength is not found in feeling nothing, but in knowing where to take what you feel.

Today, you can acknowledge both: the pride and the worry, and place them in God's hands.

Prayer
Lord, thank You for the purpose You have placed in my child's life. Today, I bring both my pride and my worries before You. Protect them, guide them, and watch over

them at all times. Help me trust You as I rest in Your care.
Amen.

Declaration
I trust God above what I feel.

**Today, I bring both my pride and my concerns to You
for my child:**

Day 11

When the Heart Learns to Trust Each Day

Proverbs 3:5-6
"Trust in the Lord with all your heart and lean not on your own understanding; in all your ways submit to Him, and He will make your paths straight."

Trusting God does not always happen once and for all. There are days when trust comes easily, and there are days when you have to remind yourself again and again.

Trust is not just a feeling—it is a daily practice. It is choosing, even when your mind wants to drift toward worry, to return to the truth that God is in control. It is saying once more, "Lord, I trust You," even when your heart is still learning.

God does not expect perfect trust. He honors consistent trust. Every time you choose to trust, even with doubts, you are growing.

Today, you do not need to have perfect faith. You simply need to take one more step in trusting.

Prayer

Lord, teach me to trust You each day. Even when my mind doubts or my heart feels uneasy, help me return to Your truth. I place my child's life in Your hands and trust that You are guiding them at all times. Amen.

Declaration

Today, I take one more step in trusting God.

Today, I place my trust in You for my child:

Day 12

When a Mother's Love Becomes Prayer

Romans 12:12
"Be joyful in hope, patient in affliction, faithful in prayer."

There comes a moment in a mother's life when love can no longer be expressed in the same way it once was. When children were young, that love showed up in hugs, constant care, and attention to every detail. But as a child grows and begins to serve far away, many of those expressions begin to change.

So, love looks for another way to stay close. And many times, that way becomes prayer.

Praying for your child is not a small reaction or a last resort. It is one of the deepest ways to love when you can no longer be present in every moment. Every thought you have about your child can become a prayer. Every worry can be turned into surrender. Every memory can become a blessing spoken before God.

You may not always have elaborate words. Some days, all you can say is, "Lord, take care of them." But even that simple prayer comes from a real love—and God hears it.

A mother's prayer reaches where her arms cannot. It crosses distance, moves through silence, and rises before God as an expression of faith and love.

Today, if your mind keeps going back to your child, do not judge yourself for it. Instead, turn that thought into prayer.

What feels heavy in your heart can become a conversation
with God.

And while you are praying here,
God is still working there.

Prayer

Lord, thank You because I can bring my child before You
again and again. Take every thought I have about them
and turn it into a prayer that reaches Your presence.
Protect them, guide them, and surround them with Your
peace. Amen.

Declaration

My love becomes prayer.

Today, I lift my child to You in prayer:

Day 13

When You Need to Rest
from Thinking So Much

Isaiah 26:3
"You will keep in perfect peace those whose minds are steadfast, because they trust in You."

There are days when nothing bad has happened, yet your mind feels exhausted. Not because of what occurred, but because of everything you have been thinking. Thoughts that come, return, repeat, and do not seem to go away. The mind analyzes, imagines, anticipates, tries to prevent—and without realizing it, it ends up exhausting the heart.

This happens often to a mother who loves deeply. Love wants to protect, and when it cannot do so through presence, it often tries to do something else: think without stopping. But overthinking does not always bring clarity. Many times, it only increases the emotional weight and steals the peace you need.

God did not create you to live in a constant state of mental tension. He also wants to give you rest in that part of your life that no one sees—your thoughts. That is why this verse speaks not only of trust, but also of peace. A complete peace that guards the mind when it learns to return to God.

Resting from thinking so much does not mean you love your child any less. It means allowing God to carry what your mind has been trying to hold on its own. It means shifting your focus. Instead of staying trapped in repetitive thoughts, you can direct your heart back to the truth that God is still caring for your child, even now.

Today, give yourself permission to rest mentally. You do not have to solve with your mind what only God can hold with His hand. Your child is in His care—and your mind can find rest there too.

Prayer

Lord, my mind sometimes fills with thoughts that exhaust me. Today, I give You everything I have been trying to carry on my own. Fill my mind with Your peace and help me rest in You. Watch over my child and teach me to trust You as I release what I cannot control. Amen.

Declaration

My mind rests in God.

Today, I place my thoughts in Your hands for my child:

Day 14

When You Remember That God Loves Your Child More Than You Do

Jeremiah 31:3
"I have loved you with an everlasting love; therefore, I have continued my faithfulness to you."

There is a truth that can be difficult to fully embrace, yet it brings a deep kind of rest: God loves your child even more than you do. As a mother, your love is strong, protective, and constant. You want to shield them from pain, from danger, from anything that could hurt them. That desire comes from the deepest place in your heart. And still, God's love reaches further than yours ever could.

God does not love your child only because they are yours. He loves them because they are His. He knew them before you ever held them for the first time. He has been present in every stage of their life, in every decision, in every step they have taken. Even in the moments when you could not be there, God was.

Sometimes we think we are the ones who care the most, who watch the most closely, who feel the most deeply. But there is a greater care—one that is more constant and more perfect than our own. God does not grow tired, He is not distracted, and He never loses sight of those He loves.

Today, you can rest in this truth: your child is not sustained by your love alone, but by the everlasting love of God. And that love does not fail, does not weaken, and does not depend on circumstances.

Prayer

Lord, thank You because You love my child even more than I ever could. Today, I rest in Your love and in Your faithfulness. Protect them, guide them, and surround them with Your presence at all times. Amen.

Declaration

God loves my child more than I ever could.

Today, I rest my child in Your love:

Day 15

When You Need to Remember
That God Is His Protector

Psalm 121:7–8
"The Lord will keep you from all harm—He will watch over your life; the Lord will watch over your coming and going both now and forevermore."

As a mother, there is a part of your heart that always wants to protect. From the time they were little, you paid attention to everything—that they would not fall, that they would not get hurt, that they would be okay. That instinct does not disappear as they grow. It simply changes the way it shows up.

When your child is far away, that desire to protect can feel even stronger, because you can no longer step in the same way. You cannot be there physically to make sure everything is okay. And that can create a sense of vulnerability.

But there is a truth that holds your heart steady: you are not the only one caring for your child.

God is his protector.

Not only at certain moments, not only when you pray, but at all times. He watches over his going out and his coming in, his decisions, his paths—even the moments you cannot see or know. His protection does not depend on your closeness, but on His constant presence.

Today, you can release a little of that weight of trying to cover everything. God is already covering what you cannot reach. Your child is not unprotected. He is under the care of a God who watches over him at all times.

Prayer

Lord, today I recognize that You are my child's protector. Watch over every step he takes, guard his life, and be with him at all times. Help me rest in Your protection and trust that You are with him. Amen.

Declaration

God protects my child at all times.

Today, I entrust my child to Your protection:

Day 16

When Your Heart Needs to Remember That God Is Still Working

Romans 8:28
"And we know that in all things God works for the good of those who love Him, who have been called according to His purpose."

There are moments when you do not see anything. No clear signs, no answers, no visible evidence of what God is doing. Everything feels quiet... or even uncertain. And in that silence, your heart can begin to wonder if everything is truly okay.

But just because you cannot see God working does not mean He has stopped.

God does not only work when there are visible signs. He also works in the hidden—in what we do not understand, in processes we cannot see from our perspective. While you are thinking, waiting, or even worrying, God is still moving on behalf of your child.

He is taking care of details you do not know about. He is opening paths you cannot anticipate. He is intervening in moments you may never even realize happened.

As a mother, it is natural to want to see in order to feel peace. But there is a deeper peace that comes when you choose to trust, even when you do not see.

Today, you can remember this: God has not stopped working in your child's life. Even now, He is present guiding, protecting, and working in all that you cannot control.

Prayer

Lord, even when I do not see what You are doing, today I choose to trust that You are working in my child's life. Watch over them, guide them, and make a way before them. Help me rest in Your work, even when I do not understand it. Amen.

Declaration

God is working in my child's life, even when I do not see it.

Today, I trust Your work in my child's life:

Day 17

When the Heart Learns to Rest in God

Psalm 62:1
"Truly my soul finds rest in God; my salvation comes from Him."

After so many thoughts, prayers, emotions, and moments of uncertainty, a deeper need begins to surface: the need to rest.

Not just physical rest, but rest for the soul. A place where your heart is no longer on constant alert, where your mind stops racing, and where worry begins to lose its grip.

That kind of rest is not found in having all the answers. It is not found in knowing exactly what is happening at every moment.

It is found in God.

Resting in God does not mean everything is resolved. It means you have chosen to trust the One who holds everything in His hands. It is allowing your soul to lean on a truth greater than your thoughts: God is in control.

As a mother, your love will always remain active. You will always think, always care, always feel. But you also need moments where you simply rest in the security that not everything depends on you.

Today, you can allow yourself that rest. Not because everything is clear, but because God remains faithful.

Prayer

Lord, today I want to rest in You. I release the need to be in control and place my trust in Your hands. Watch over my child, protect them, and fill me with Your peace as I learn to rest in Your faithfulness. Amen.

Declaration

My soul rests in God.

Today, I rest my heart in You for my child:

Day 18

When Hope Returns to the Heart

Lamentations 3:21-23
"Yet this I call to mind and therefore I have hope: Because of the Lord's great love we are not consumed, for His compassions never fail."

There are days when your heart feels lighter. Not because everything has changed, or because you have more answers, but because something within you begins to rest a little more.

It is as if, for a moment, worry loosens its grip... and hope finds room to return.

Hope does not always come with big signs. Sometimes it returns quietly, almost unnoticed. It comes when you remember who God is—when you choose to believe that He is still good, faithful, and present, even in the middle of uncertainty.

As a mother, it is easy for your heart to lean toward fear. But it is also true that it can learn to return to hope again and again.

Not because you ignore reality, but because you choose to see that reality through the faithfulness of God.

Today, if you feel even a small sense of rest, embrace it. Do not question it. Do not interrupt it with doubtful thoughts.

Allow hope to take its place in your heart again.

Prayer

Lord, thank You because Your love never runs out. Today,
I allow hope to return to my heart. Help me trust in Your
faithfulness and rest in the assurance that You are caring
for my child at all times. Amen.

Declaration

Hope lives in my heart because God is faithful.

Today, I receive Your hope for my child:

Day 19

When a Mother's Love Continues to Accompany

Isaiah 66:13

"As a mother comforts her child, so will I comfort you; and you will be comforted."

Even when your child is far away, there is something that never breaks: the bond that connects you.

A mother's love does not depend on distance. It does not weaken with miles, and it does not disappear with time. It remains present, active, and close in ways that are often difficult to explain.

You may not be able to hold them today. You may not be able to see them or speak with them at every moment. But your love is still there.

In every prayer, in every thought, in every memory, in every moment you bring them before God, you are still accompanying them in a real and meaningful way.

And even more beautiful than that is knowing that God is also present. He is not only with your child—He is with you as well. He comforts, sustains, and understands everything in your heart.

You are not alone in this process. Neither you nor your child are walking through this alone.

Today, you can rest in this truth: love is not limited by distance. It continues to reach, to cover, and to connect.

Prayer

Lord, thank You because the love I have for my child continues to reach them even from a distance. Comfort me when I need it, and remind me that You are with both of us at all times. Amen.

Declaration

My love continues to reach my child—and God does too.

Today, I hold my child in love before You:

Day 20

When You Need to Remember
That God Goes Before Him

Deuteronomy 31:8
*"The Lord Himself goes before you and will be with you;
He will never leave you nor forsake you."*

As a mother, you often find yourself thinking about the road ahead for your child. You wonder what their days will look like, what they will face, what decisions they will have to make, and what situations may come their way.

It is natural to want to get ahead, to prepare the path, to make sure everything is in place before they arrive there.

But there is something that brings deep rest: your child is never walking into the unknown alone.

God is already ahead of them.

Before your child arrives somewhere, God is already there. Before they face a situation, God has already seen it. Before they have to decide, God already knows the outcome.

He does not only walk with them—He goes before them.

This means there is no path that is unprepared, no step outside of His knowledge, and no moment that catches Him by surprise.

Today, you can release the weight of trying to anticipate everything. God is already preparing what lies ahead. And your child is walking toward a place where God's presence is already waiting.

Prayer

Lord, thank You because You go before my child. Prepare every path, guide every step, and be with them at all times. Help me rest in knowing that You are already where they are going. Amen.

Declaration

God goes before my child at all times.

Today, I trust You with what lies ahead for my child:

Day 21

A Mother Never Prays Alone

Matthew 18:20
"For where two or three gather in My name, there am I with them."

Throughout this journey, you have prayed many times—quietly, in a whisper, perhaps with tears, or in the middle of your daily routines.

And even though at times it may have felt like you were alone in those moments, the truth is different.

You never pray alone.

God is with you in every prayer. He hears every word, even the ones you cannot fully express. He knows the intention of your heart, the depth of your love, and the weight of your thoughts.

Every prayer you have lifted for your child has been heard. Not one has been lost. Not one has been ignored.

And you are not the only mother praying. There are many others, in different places, with the same love and the same faith, lifting prayers for their children who serve.

There is an unseen network of faith, love, and intercession.

And in the middle of it all, God is still working.

Today, you can close this time with a steady confidence: your prayers matter, they carry weight, and they reach heaven.

You are not alone. You never have been.

Prayer

Lord, thank You because You always hear my prayers. Today, I once again place my child's life in Your hands. Protect them, guide them, and be with them at all times. Thank You because I am not alone, and because You are always with me. Amen.

Declaration

I never pray alone—God always hears me.

Today, I place my child before You once again:

Verses for Urgent Moments

There are moments when your heart races, your mind will not slow down, and peace feels far away. In those moments, you may not have the strength to read an entire devotional—but you can still hold on to a truth.

This list is for those moments.

When you do not know what to think, read.
When you do not know what to say, declare.
When you do not know what to do, come back to these verses.

When you feel anxious
Philippians 4:6–7
"Do not be anxious about anything... and the peace of God, which surpasses all understanding, will guard your hearts."

———

When your mind imagines the worst
2 Corinthians 10:5
"...we take captive every thought to make it obedient to Christ."

———

When you have no news about your child
Psalm 121:4
"He who watches over Israel will neither slumber nor sleep."

———

When you feel afraid
Isaiah 41:10
"Do not fear, for I am with you..."

When you need to remember that God protects them
Psalm 121:7-8
"The Lord will keep you from all harm..."

When the news unsettles your heart
Psalm 112:7
"They will have no fear of bad news..."

When you feel emotionally exhausted
Matthew 11:28
"Come to Me, all you who are weary and burdened, and I will give you rest."

When you need to let go of control
1 Peter 5:7
"Cast all your anxiety on Him because He cares for you."

When you need to remember God is with your child
Joshua 1:9
"The Lord your God will be with you wherever you go."

When you need peace in your mind
Isaiah 26:3
"You will keep in perfect peace those whose minds are steadfast..."

When you want to trust again
Proverbs 3:5–6
"Trust in the Lord with all your heart..."

When you need hope
Lamentations 3:22–23
"The Lord's great love never fails..."

Come back to this page whenever your heart needs it.

Final Prayer of a Mother

Lord,

Today I come before You with everything in my heart—my love, my worries, my thoughts, and even the things I do not always know how to express. You know every emotion, every concern, and every moment my mind has tried to run ahead of what it cannot control.

I place my child's life in Your hands once again—not as an act of desperation, but as an act of trust. I recognize that You love them more than I ever could, that You see them even when I cannot, and that Your care does not depend on my closeness, but on Your constant presence.

Lord, watch over every step they take. Protect them at all times. Surround them with Your peace, guide their decisions, and guard their life wherever they are. Be their refuge in difficult moments and their strength in every challenge.

And as You care for them, care for me as well.

Guard my mind from thoughts that steal my peace. Teach me to rest in You, to trust in Your faithfulness, and to release what is not mine to carry. When silence unsettles me, remind me that You are present. When anxiety tries to take hold, fill me with Your peace.

Today, I choose to trust.

I trust that You are working.
I trust that You are caring.
I trust that You never leave us alone.

Thank You for hearing every prayer, even the ones I cannot
fully put into words.

Into Your hands I place my child...
and my heart as well.

Amen.

Conclusion

If you have made it this far, I want you to know something.

You are not alone.

Maybe no one sees everything that goes through your mind. Maybe you do not say out loud every worry, every thought, every "what if..." that shows up in the quiet moments. But God sees it—and He also sees your love.

You have prayed more than others know. You have trusted even when it has been difficult. You have kept going, even with a restless heart.

And that... is also faith.

Not a perfect faith, not a doubt-free faith, but a real one. A faith that rises, that persists, that keeps returning to God again and again.

As a sister, I want to tell you this with all my heart: you are doing well.

Loving like this is not easy. Letting go like this is not easy. Trusting when you cannot see is not easy.

But here you are.

And while you keep praying, God keeps working.

You do not have to do this perfectly. You do not need to have all the answers. You only need to keep bringing your child before God... again and again.

There will be calmer days and harder ones. Days when peace flows, and others when your mind starts racing again. And in all of those days, God remains the same.

Faithful. Present. Near.

So, when this book comes to an end, your prayer does not.

Keep talking to God.
Keep surrendering.
Keep trusting.

And when your heart feels tight again... come back.

Come back to these verses.
Come back to this prayer.
Come back to that place where God reminds you that He is in control.

I embrace you from a distance.

And I pray with you.

About the Author

Ivelisse **Adorno** is a woman of faith, writer, and guide through emotional and spiritual journeys. Her heart is drawn to women who love deeply, yet quietly carry concerns they do not always know how to express.

This devotional was born from a real experience: witnessing up close the heart of a mother who prays for her child while they serve far away. From that place, Ivelisse writes not as someone who has all the answers, but as someone who firmly believes that God is the One who sustains, cares for, and walks with us—even in the most uncertain moments.

Through her writing, she seeks to create spaces of rest, reflection, and encounter with God, where faith is not presented as perfection, but as a daily decision to trust.

About Kitvi Editorial, LLC

Kitvi Editorial, LLC is an independent publishing imprint dedicated to creating books that nourish the heart, the mind, and the spirit.

Each publication is developed with the purpose of walking alongside real-life journeys, integrating faith, reflection, and practical tools that help readers find clarity, rest, and direction.

More than books, Kitvi Editorial, LLC creates resources that remain.